HARD NUTS
OF HISTORY

Ancient
Egypt

TRACEY TURNER

ILLUSTRATED BY JAMIE LENMAN

First published 2014 by
A & C Black, an imprint of Bloomsbury Publishing Plc
50 Bedford Square, London WC1B 3DP

www.bloomsbury.com

Bloomsbury is a registered trademark of Bloomsbury Publishing Plc

ISBN 978-1-4729-0563-5

A CIP catalogue for this book is available from the British Library.

This book is produced using paper that is made from wood
grown in managed, sustainable forests. It is natural, renewable and
recyclable. The logging and manufacturing processes conform
to the environmental regulations of the country of origin.

Printed in China by Leo Paper Products, Heshan, Guangdong

1 3 5 7 9 10 8 6 4 2

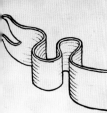

CONTENTS

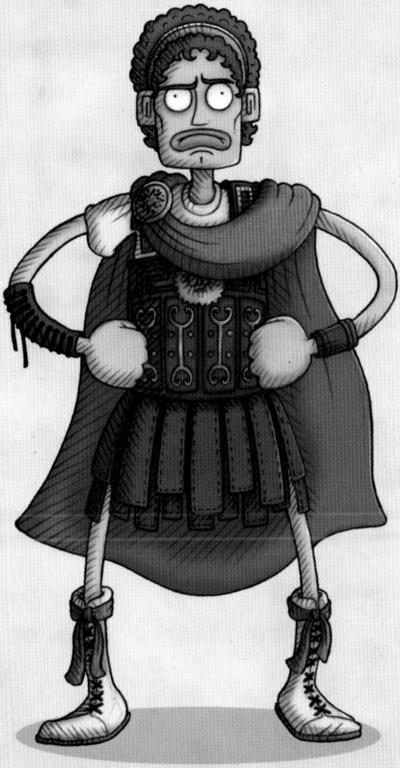

INTRODUCTION

This book contains some of the hardest nuts of ancient Egypt, from powerful pharaohs to rampaging invaders. Some of them were brave warriors, some were worshipped as gods, and most of them were made into mummies. But all of them were as hard as nails.

FIND OUT ABOUT . . .

- Mummified crocodiles

- The Book of the Dead

- Amazing animal-headed gods

- The dark and mysterious secrets of the pyramids

If you've ever wanted to drive a war chariot, invade Nubia, or live forever, read on. Follow the hard nuts across the Sinai desert, along the River Nile, and into a swirling Saharan sandstorm.

As well as discovering stories of courage and cunning, you might be in for a few surprises. Did you know, for example, that Tutankhamun's heart is missing? Or that King Cambyses misplaced an entire army in Egypt?

You're about to meet some of the toughest people of ancient Egypt . . .

Plus play the game on page 36 and see if you can make your way through the Egyptian underworld to the goal of everlasting life!

CLEOPATRA

Cleopatra was an ambitious pharaoh who became one of the most famous women in the whole of history.

HARD NUT RATING: 7.8

LITTLE BROTHER

Cleopatra was a member of the Ptolemy Dynasty. She became pharaoh in 51 BC, ruling alongside her little brother, Ptolemy. She had to marry Ptolemy, which was bad enough, but Cleopatra couldn't stand the idea of sharing power. She stamped Egyptian coins with her own image but not Ptolemy's, and left his name off official documents. Cleopatra made some powerful enemies in her time, and in 48 BC she was driven out of the country. Little brother Ptolemy became the sole pharaoh, even though he was still only 13.

ROME AND EGYPT

But Cleopatra wasn't going without a fight and got help from Julius Caesar, one of the most powerful men in the world: he was in charge of the mighty Roman Empire. Caesar fell in love with Cleopatra and backed her claim to the throne. Together they defeated Ptolemy, and Cleopatra became pharaoh again – though she *still* had to rule with a brother, Ptolemy XIV this time. But she spent most of her time in Rome with Caesar anyway, where they had their son, Caesarion. In 44 BC Caesar was assassinated, and Cleopatra went back to Egypt. Ptolemy XIV didn't last

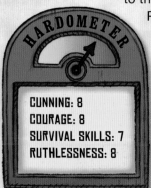

HARDOMETER

CUNNING: 8
COURAGE: 8
SURVIVAL SKILLS: 7
RUTHLESSNESS: 8

long after that – Cleopatra probably had him poisoned so she could rule with her son, Caesarion.

ANOTHER ROMAN BOYFRIEND

Not long after Caesar's death Cleopatra found another powerful Roman boyfriend, Mark Antony, who was one of the three new rulers of Rome. Together, Cleopatra and Mark Antony declared that Caesarion, Cleopatra and Caesar's son, was the true ruler of Rome (making Cleopatra and Mark Antony the most powerful people in the world). Understandably, the other Roman rulers were upset, and declared war. Mark Antony fought a battle at sea with one of them, Octavian.

DISASTER

Unfortunately for Cleopatra and Mark Antony, the battle at sea was a total disaster for Antony. He killed himself afterwards, and so did Cleopatra – the story goes that she let a venomous snake, an asp, bite her, and died of the poison. Caesarion was killed on Octavian's orders, and Octavian went on to become Rome's first emperor.

KING NARMER

Narmer was an ancient warrior king who conquered the whole of Egypt and made it one united country for the first time.

HARD NUT RATING: 8.8

UPPER AND LOWER

By the time King Narmer lived, around 3200 BC, people had been living in Egypt's rich, fertile land for thousands of years. Egypt was divided into Upper Egypt, the southern part, and Lower Egypt, the northern part. Each kingdom had its own king – King Narmer wore the white crown of Upper Egypt, while the King of Lower Egypt wore a red crown. The crowns were also used in pictures as symbols of the two kingdoms.

THE NARMER PALETTE

Five thousand years is a long time ago, so what we know about King Narmer is based on just a few ancient documents, including one of the first historical documents in the whole world, the Narmer Palette. Palettes were used in ancient Egypt for mixing cosmetics – everyone wore make-up, including men, women and children. The Narmer Palette is special because it's very big (it was probably used for ceremonies in a temple), and because it tells a story.

SMITING

On one side of the palette there's a picture of Narmer, wearing the crown of Upper Egypt and holding an enemy by the hair, about to bash him with a mace (this is known as the 'smiting pose' – the Egyptians did a lot of smiting). On the other side of the palette Narmer is marching towards naked, headless enemies wearing the crown of

Lower Egypt. There are two obvious conclusions that can be taken from this palette: first of all, Narmer had done a lot of smiting, and second of all, the people he'd bashed were the Lower Egyptians, owing to his new crown.

EGYPT UNITED

Narmer's conquering meant that the unified country could become better organised, grow richer, and have a permanent professional army, which could go off smiting people at a moment's notice. Narmer built an impressive new capital city, Memphis, which is around 20 kilometres south of the modern city of Cairo. He had created a country that would be a mighty empire for thousands of years.

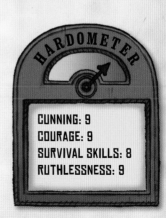

HARDOMETER

CUNNING: 9
COURAGE: 9
SURVIVAL SKILLS: 8
RUTHLESSNESS: 9

A BRIEF HISTORY OF ANCIENT EGYPT

Ancient Egyptian history can be very confusing – it was such a long time ago, and there's an awful lot of it to try and understand. Here's a quick and simple version.*

THE FIRST EGYPTIANS

In the dim and distant past (maybe 9,500 years ago), people began to settle in Egypt. As the climate became drier, they moved towards the fertile lands next to the River Nile, while the rest of the area became a desert.

THE OLD KINGDOM

Egyptian history is divided into kingdoms: the Old Kingdom, Middle Kingdom and New Kingdom. There are also periods when things weren't quite so straightforward in between these three kingdoms. By around 3200 BC, Egypt was united into one country and ruled by pharaohs, from the capital city at Memphis. During the Old Kingdom,

the biggest pyramids and the Great Sphinx were built. After the Old Kingdom, there was a period of about 130 years when minor kings controlled Egypt, known as the Intermediate Period.

THE MIDDLE KINGDOM

The capital city was moved to Thebes, in southern Egypt, during the Middle Kingdom, and Egypt conquered Nubia, to the south of the country. The Middle Kingdom lasted around 250 years before the ruling dynasty was interrupted, and there was another (Second) Intermediate Period. Then, in 1663 BC, Asian invaders called the Hyksos conquered Egypt and ruled from their capital at Avaris in the eastern Nile delta.

THE NEW KINGDOM

The Hyksos were eventually chucked out, and the New Kingdom was founded in 1550 BC. The New Kingdom pharaohs stopped building pyramids and started building their royal tombs in the Valley of the Kings. This is the period when Hatshepsut, Tutankhamun and Ramesses the Great (among others) were pharaohs of Egypt.

AFTER THE NEW KINGDOM

Egypt became part of the Persian Empire in 525 BC, then it was conquered by Alexander the Great about 200 years later. About 30 years after that Ptolemy I began his dynasty of Ptolemies, which lasted until the Romans conquered Egypt in 30 BC.

* There's also a timeline on page 58.

RAMESSES THE GREAT

Ramesses II is one of the most famous pharaohs of Egypt. He battled the Hittites, signed the world's first peace treaty, and ruled for more than 60 years.

APPRENTICE PHARAOH

Ramesses' dad, the pharaoh Seti I, had been preparing him for kingship from an early age and made him captain of the army when Ramesses was just ten years old. Ramesses took part in several battles with Seti, who liked a good fight. Ramesses began his long reign as pharaoh when his father died.

SORTING OUT THE HITTITES

Seti had waged war on various people in the Middle East, including the Hittites, whose empire included some of the land that used to belong to Egypt – Seti won some of the land back, but then lost it again. Ramesses decided to sort out the Hittites once and for all. In 1274 BC, he led his army to Kadesh, the Hittite stronghold. The battle that took place was one of the earliest recorded battles, and the biggest chariot battle ever. Thousands of chariots, as well as cavalry and infantry, took part in the fight, which turned out to be very bloody indeed. Ramesses recorded the battle as a glorious victory for the Egyptians, but we know

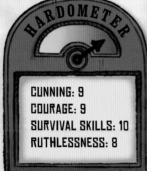

HARDOMETER

CUNNING: 9
COURAGE: 9
SURVIVAL SKILLS: 10
RUTHLESSNESS: 8

from other records that the result was a draw – Ramesses hadn't captured Kadesh yet.

PEACE AT LAST

In the following years Ramesses kept trying to conquer the Hittites. After 16 years the Hittites and the Egyptians agreed a peace treaty – the world's first. But just because Egypt had established one peace treaty, it didn't mean Ramesses was going to stop fighting: he waged war with other people instead, including the Libyans, who unwisely tried to settle by the river Nile.

RAMESSES' LEGACY

Ramesses built lots of temples and other impressive buildings – the most famous is at Abu Simnel, and includes four giant statues of Ramesses himself – and made sure his name, image and glorious deeds were written all over them. He died an old man, probably in his 90s, and had more than a hundred children with lots of different wives. He was buried in the Valley of the Kings, and his mummy has survived the centuries: it's now in the Cairo Museum.

PHABULOUS PHARAOHS

Not only was the pharaoh the most important person in Egypt, but he or she was also worshipped as a god.

Not surprisingly, pharaohs weren't known for being modest – they were always spouting about how great they were, and how they were (literally) divine. And their boasting lasted for centuries – they tended to carve their great exploits onto buildings and monuments. Below are some phabulous pharaoh facts.

• The pharaoh was kept pretty busy with things like making laws, commanding the army (and sometimes fighting with it), handling the country's finances, building great monuments, and being the high priest.

• The word 'pharaoh' comes from the Egyptian word *per-aa*, meaning palace or great house. Eventually a pharaoh wasn't just the name of the palace, but also the person who lived in it.

• Pharaohs often had a number of wives (though female pharaohs tended only to have one husband). At least one of those wives might be a sister, or even a daughter. The idea was that marrying within the royal family strengthened the king's claim to rule. And perhaps the pharaohs were following the ways of the Egyptian gods, who married sisters and daughters – after all, the pharaohs believed themselves to be gods.

- Pharaohs had special symbols of royalty:

Double crown: called the pschent, which stood for the two kingdoms of Upper and Lower Egypt united. The white section at the top stood for Upper Egypt, and the red section symbolised Lower Egypt.

Crook: (like the stick that a shepherd uses) and flail (like a whip), which were emblems of the god Osiris and stood for kingship and the fertile Egyptian land.

False beard: They wore a false beard – even the female pharaohs!

Ankh: This was the symbol of life, and the holder of an ankh held the power of life and death. Only the pharaoh was allowed to carry one.

- After a pharaoh died, the idea was that he would take his place among the gods, which was one of the reasons a pharaoh's funeral and tomb were so elaborate.

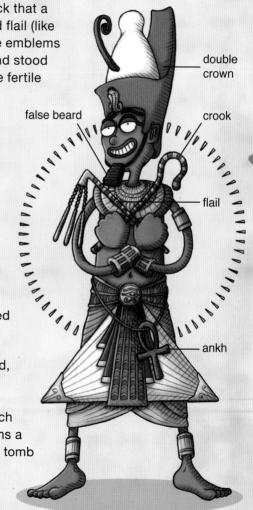

double crown

false beard

crook

flail

ankh

SEQENENRE THE BRAVE

Seqenenre was a king of Upper Egypt who rebelled against his foreign overlords, and was badly battered in the process.

UPPER EGYPTIAN KING

Seqenenre was king of Egypt around the middle of the 1500s BC, ruling from the city of Thebes in Upper Egypt, near the modern Egyptian city of Luxor. By the time he was pharaoh, Hyksos kings had been ruling Lower Egypt – the north of the country – for around a hundred years.

HYKSOS OVERLORDS

The Hyksos were foreigners from Asia who had settled in Egypt's Nile delta during the 1700s BC, and ended up ruling most of Lower Egypt. Although the Hyksos allowed an Egyptian king to rule Upper Egypt, they were the overlords of Upper Egypt as well. They might have managed to defeat the Egyptians because they had better equipment: they introduced horse-drawn chariots and weapons such as bows and battle axes.

HARDOMETER

CUNNING: 8
COURAGE: 9
SURVIVAL SKILLS: 5
RUTHLESSNESS: 8

SEQENENRE'S HIPPOS

We know that Seqenenre's kingship was under the rule of the Hyksos because of part of a story, written later. It says that Apopis, the Hyksos king, sent a message to Seqenenre asking him to remove the hippopotamuses from their pool at Thebes, because the noise they made was keeping him awake in his palace, which was hundreds of miles away. Either ancient Egyptian hippos were monstrous beasts with an incredibly loud roar, or Apopis was making a joke – or the point was that he could tell Seqenenre to do whatever he liked. The rest of the story is lost, but Seqenenre must have been getting fed up with Apopis, because during his rule the Egyptians started to rebel against Hyksos rule.

HYKSOS GO HOME

Seqenenre started a military campaign that would finally see the back of the Hyksos. Seqenenre's mummy shows severe head injuries, including three vicious axe wounds, a massive bash of some kind, and a sword or spear wound. The mummy is evidence that Seqenenre died violently – possibly while fighting the Hyksos. Experts have argued that he was either killed in battle, assassinated while he slept, or executed. Seqenenre didn't manage to get rid of the Hyksos, but his successors (the people who ruled after him) finally drove them out for good.

MAKING MUMMIES

The first Egyptian mummies were made naturally when the dead were buried in the hot desert sand: the bodies' fluids would drain away and the corpses were preserved in the sand. When people started putting the dead inside coffins, they rotted, so the Egyptians cleverly worked out a way of preserving the dead artificially.

Preserving the body was important to the Egyptians because they believed that people's souls went on a journey to the underworld when they died, where they were judged; if that went well, the soul and the body were reunited and lived forever. But the soul had to recognise its body in order for this to happen. The body had to look just as it did in life and so it was really important that bodies were embalmed carefully.

There were different levels of mummification depending on cost. Here's the deluxe version:

YOU'RE NEXT.

1. Extract the brain through the nose using a special hook. To do this, wiggle the hook about, then let the brain drain out into a bowl. Chuck out the brains for the hungry jackals.

2. Remove all internal organs and put them in special canopic jars. Return the heart to the body (it has to be weighed when Osiris judges the dead person).

3. Dry the body with salts – this takes 40 days.

4. Treat the dried body with oils and resins.

5. Hairdressers and beauticians make the body appear as lifelike as possible.

6. Wrap the body in many metres of linen.

7. Cover the body in lucky charms and place in the coffin with the Book of the Dead.

8. Fit the funeral mask.

The funeral ceremonies were designed to reactivate the soul.

ANIMAL MUMMIES

Animals were also made into mummies. Animals associated with a particular god (there were lots of animal gods) would be mummified and offered in the god's temple. There were lots of cats offered to the goddess Bastet (see page 31). Crocodiles were mummified and offered to the crocodile god, Sobek. Other mummified animals include rams, ibises, baboons and jackals. Pet dogs and cats were often mummified too and buried with their owners.

MUMMY PARTY

Some Egyptian mummies suffered dreadful fates. During the 19th century, rich tourists would bring back a mummy as a souvenir. Then they'd have a mummy unwrapping party at home.

KING PIYE

Kushite warrior King Piye took control of Egypt in the 700s BC, and laid the foundations for a new Egyptian dynasty.

HARD NUT RATING: 9

KUSHITE KING

Piye was King of Kush, a kingdom to the south of Egypt that was part of Nubia in ancient Egyptian times, but is now part of Sudan. By the time Piye was king, Egypt wasn't ruled by a single pharaoh. The country had split into different territories with lots of different rulers.

EGYPTIAN INVASION

King Piye had plans for expansion and so took his army north, attacking as he went. Within the first ten years of becoming king he'd conquered Upper Egypt. Piye's sister, Amenirdis, became an important priestess known as the God's Wife of Amun (the god Amun was a special favourite of Piye's). It wasn't just a religious job, though. Amenirdis's new role meant that the area around the city of Thebes, previously controlled by Egyptian pharaoh Osorkon III, now came under Piye's control as well.

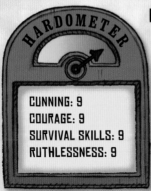

HARDOMETER

CUNNING: 9
COURAGE: 9
SURVIVAL SKILLS: 9
RUTHLESSNESS: 9

ENEMY ALLIES

Meanwhile, further north, Tefnakht, ruler of one of the kingdoms of the Nile delta, was getting jumpy – King Piye was getting far too powerful. So he formed an alliance with a group of other kings of the Nile delta against King Piye, and they prepared their united army to meet him. But the alliance wasn't tough enough for Piye, who marched north and battered the alliance at Heracliopolis. Then he captured the cities of Hermopolis and Memphis, the ancient Egyptian capital, for good measure.

NEW DYNASTY

Now King Piye was ruler of Lower Egypt as well as Upper Egypt. Tefnakht ran away, and the other Nile delta rulers submitted to Piye, who took the treasure and animals they offered, celebrated his victory, then went back to Nubia (he must have preferred it there). Even though he wasn't physically there, Piye ruled Egypt for more than 30 years, until he died in 716 BC. Piye had never made himself pharaoh of Egypt, but after his death his brother Shabaka took control of Egypt and became the first pharaoh of the 25th dynasty.

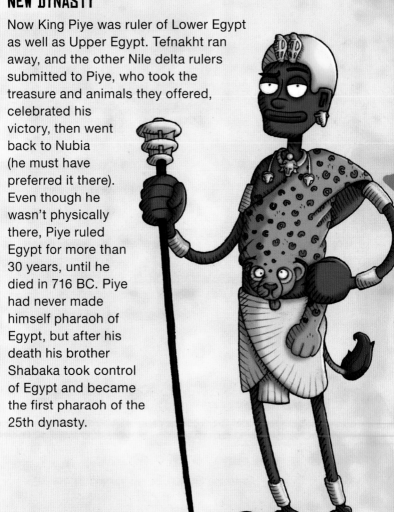

TUTANKHAMUN

The pharaoh Tutankhamun's life was a short one, and yet he's probably the most famous pharaoh of them all.

BOY KING

Tutankhamun became king after the death of Akhenaten when he was was only eight or nine years old. He might have been the son of Akhenaten, though no one knows for sure. When Akhenaten was in power he had replaced the traditional gods of worship with worship of the sun god Aten.

However, Tutankhamun's rule put things back the way they were. According to documents from Tutankhamun's reign, the reforms had left the country in chaos because the traditional gods had been cross and abandoned Egypt. He moved the capital from Akhetaten back to Memphis.

KING TUT'S TOMB

More than 3,000 years later, in 1922, the archaeologist Howard Carter discovered King Tutankhamun's tomb in the Valley of the Kings, after years of searching for it. It was one of the most exciting Egyptian discoveries ever, because unlike all the other tombs in the Valley of the Kings, Tutankhamun's tomb had not been raided by treasure hunters. When Carter entered it, it was exactly as it had been left. It contained Tutankhamun's mummy, caskets, beautiful golden mask, chariots, jewellery, weapons, furniture and other treasures.

SUDDEN DEATH

Tutankhamun had died suddenly aged about 17. No one is sure how he died, and lots of different reasons have been suggested – disease, perhaps malaria, a hunting accident, or assassination. The most intriguing suggestion is that he died in battle, run over by a chariot – the left side of his mummified body is very badly injured, with a big chunk of his pelvis completely missing. Egyptian mummies almost always have their hearts placed back inside the mummified body, but Tutankhamun's is missing. Perhaps it was too badly damaged to be used.

AY AY

Tutankhamun's successor was called Ay. He had been Tutankhamun's adviser and probably his regent when he was very young. It's been suggested that he took the tomb intended for Tutankhamun for himself. Tutankhamun's smaller tomb was buried, probably after a flood.

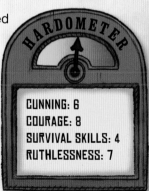

HARDOMETER

CUNNING: 6
COURAGE: 8
SURVIVAL SKILLS: 4
RUTHLESSNESS: 7

THE VALLEY OF THE KINGS

After 1550 BC, the capital of Egypt moved from Memphis, in Upper Egypt, to Thebes, in Lower Egypt, and marked the beginning of what's known as the New Kingdom. The New Kingdom pharaohs still wanted impressive tombs for themselves, but they had realised that building pyramids to house their dead bodies was a bit like putting up a massive sign to robbers that said 'Treasure Inside'. So they started building secret underground tombs instead.

• The tombs were built on the opposite side of the River Nile from Thebes, in the cliffs on the edge of the desert. The sun set behind the cliffs, which tied in with the idea that the pharaoh would meet the sun god after death.

• There were three main burial sites near Thebes: the Valley of the Nobles, the Valley of the Queens, and the Valley of the Kings.

• The tombs were full of all the things the dead person might need in the afterlife, including furniture, clothes, jewellery, food and drink, and even pets (baboons and gazelles, as well as cats and dogs, have been found).

• To thwart tomb raiders, the tombs were designed with false burial chambers, perilous shafts, and secret stairways. But over the many centuries since they were built, most were robbed anyway. By the time of the Romans, most were plundered and in ruins.

• So far, 63 tombs from the New Kingdom have been discovered. Tutankhamun's tomb is the only one that hadn't already been looted when it was found by an archaeologist.

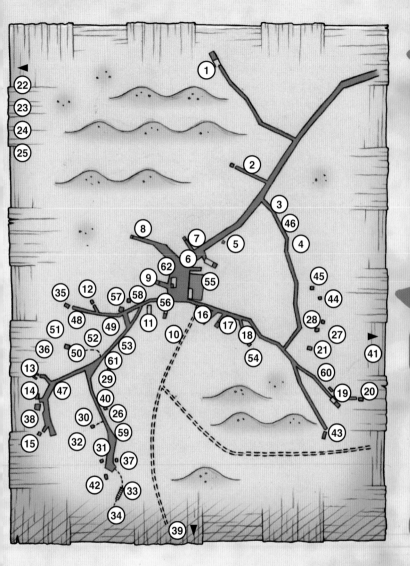

• Above is a map which shows the layout of the Valley of the Kings. Each number represents a tomb. Several of the pharaohs mentioned in this book are buried in these tombs, including Thutmose III (34) and Tutankhamun (62).

QUEEN NEFERTITI

Queen Nefertiti wasn't a pharaoh, but she became the most powerful woman in Egypt and one of the most famous ancient Egyptians of all.

HARD NUT
RATING: 7.3

WHAT A BEAUTY

'Nefertiti' means 'A Beautiful Woman Has Come', which is quite a name to live up to. Luckily, Queen Nefertiti did – she was famously drop-dead gorgeous. She became the Chief Royal Wife of the pharaoh Akhenaten around the middle of the 1300s BC.

SMITING

No other Egyptian queen was given the same top billing as Nefertiti had. She appears more often than Akhenaten in carvings, and she even appears smiting enemies – holding a kneeling enemy's hair while wielding a club, about to bash him. This 'smiting pose' is usually reserved for pharaohs. She had her own special crown, too. Although she was the favourite and chief wife of Akhenaten, and had six daughters with him, she shared her husband with other wives, one of whom was the mother of the famous Tutankhamum, Akhenaten's successor.

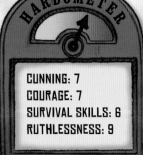

HARDOMETER

CUNNING: 7
COURAGE: 7
SURVIVAL SKILLS: 6
RUTHLESSNESS: 9

RELIGIOUS REVOLUTION

Akhenaten is famous for his attempt to change the religion of Egypt. He worshipped the sun god Aten instead of the many and various Egyptian gods, who were represented as animals, humans, or animal-headed humans (see page 30). He built a new capital city, Akhetaten (modern-day Amarna), with temples to Aten and palaces for himself.

NEFERTITI VANISHES

When Akhenaten had been pharaoh for 12 years, Nefertiti disappeared from the records. No one knows why – she might have died suddenly (though some evidence suggests she outlived her husband). Some historians believe she disappeared as queen because she became joint ruler with her husband, while others think she upset the pharaoh and so everyone stopped mentioning her. We might never know what really happened.

NEFERTITI'S HEAD

When Akhenaten died, the new capital city and its temples were abandoned. The new pharaoh went back to worshipping the old gods, and so did everyone else. Later pharaohs removed Akhenaten's name from records, because they wanted to forget about the new religion. But Nefertiti made another appearance in 1912. A beautiful ancient limestone statue of her head and shoulders was discovered. It's made her one of the most famous ancient Egyptians ever.

THE GOOD GOD GUIDE

More than 2,000 gods and goddesses were worshipped in ancient Egypt. Many of them were represented by animals, or animal-headed people. Some were more important than others. Here are a few weird and wonderful ancient Egyptian gods.

Re: God of the sun, Re was the most important god of all. He was represented as the Sun itself, or by a falcon-headed man wearing a sun-disk on his head, or sometimes in other forms, such as a scarab (a dung beetle).

Osiris: God and chief judge of the underworld, represented as a mummified pharaoh. He'd been a king who was murdered by his jealous brother, Seth.

HORUS

BASTET

Seth: Osiris's murderer, Seth was the god of violence and thunderstorms. Represented by an animal, but not a recognisable one, with a long, curved snout and long ears.

Isis: Osiris's wife and mother of Horus. She was goddess of motherhood and children, and also mourner of the dead, and protector of coffins and canopic jars.

Horus: The sky god, protector of the pharaoh. Despite his human parents (Isis and Osiris) he was represented as a falcon, or a falcon-headed man.

Anubis: Represented as a jackal-headed man or a black jackal, Anubis was the god of embalmers and guided the dead through the underworld.

Amun: Identified with Re (and sometimes worshipped as Amun-Re), Amun became the favourite god of the kings of the 18th dynasty – it's why Tutankhamun has the 'amun' bit at the end of his name. There's a huge temple to Amun built at Karnak.

Bastet: The Egyptians were fond of cats, and Bastet is the cat goddess, represented as a cat-headed woman.

Thoth: The moon god, depicted as an ibis-headed man. He was the other gods' scribe.

Hathor: The cow goddess, represented as a cow-headed woman, or a woman with a cow's horns and ears. She was a symbol of motherhood and fertility.

Aten: Aten was the sun-disk god worshipped by Akhenaten and Nefertiti (see page 28). After they died, worship of Aten died too.

PTOLEMY I

Ptolemy wasn't Egyptian at all – he was a hard-nut Macedonian general. He founded an Egyptian dynasty that lasted until the Romans conquered Egypt.

HARD NUT
RATING: 8.8

ALEXANDER'S ARMY

Ptolemy was from Macedonia, where he joined the army of Alexander the Great, the unbeatable Macedonian king who conquered a huge empire. Ptolemy was a fierce warrior and brilliant general, and eventually he was given command of the Macedonian fleet, and Alexander decorated him for his bravery and skill in battle.

DIVIDING THE EMPIRE

When Alexander died suddenly in 323 BC, there was a struggle to grab his massive empire. Ptolemy suggested that the different provinces of the empire should be divided up among Alexander's best generals – including him, of course. Back in 332 BC, Alexander had invaded Egypt, made it part of his empire, and installed his own king to rule it. Ptolemy decided he should be the new Egyptian ruler. He couldn't just put his feet up, though. First he had to defeat another of Alexander's generals, Perdiccas, who invaded in 322 BC, but was thwarted by Ptolemy's battle tactics and the River Nile, which swept away some of his soldiers.

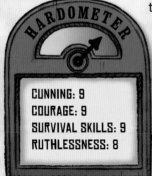

HARDOMETER

CUNNING: 9
COURAGE: 9
SURVIVAL SKILLS: 9
RUTHLESSNESS: 8

ANTIGONUS ANTAGONISES

In fact there was no rest at all for Ptolemy. Antigonus, who had also fought as a general alongside Alexander the Great, started causing trouble. He suggested – quite forcefully, and with the use of a massive army – that he should be in charge of the whole of Alexander's old empire. Ptolemy joined forces with some of the other generals who now ruled Alexander's empire. Both sides had victories and defeats, but Ptolemy managed to keep Antigonus out of Egypt, and took the title of king in 305 BC to celebrate.

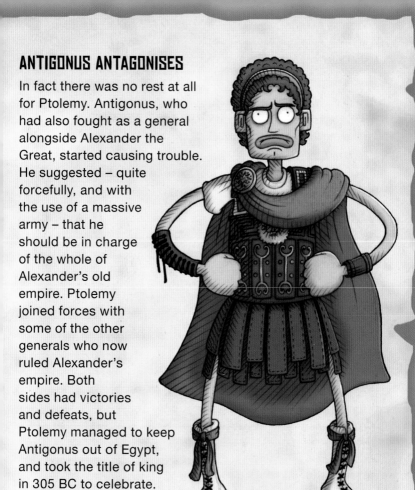

DYNASTY OF PTOLEMIES

Ptolemy had had enough of battles by this time, and, as far as he could, expanded and secured his empire by marriages and alliances rather than fighting, though he did do a bit of conquering in Cyprus and Syria. Before Ptolemy died in 283 BC he made sure that his son would succeed him – Ptolemy II was the second in a long line of Ptolemies, a dynasty that lasted hundreds of years.

THUTMOSE III

Thutmose was a warrior pharaoh who made the Egyptian Empire the largest it had ever been, and never lost a battle.

HARD NUT RATING: 9

HATSHEPSUT RULES

Thutmose became pharaoh in 1479 BC when his father, Thutmose II, died. Because he was a child, a regent ruled for him – Hatshepsut (see page 44) who was his stepmother and his father's chief wife. After a few years, Hatshepsut made herself pharaoh, so Thutmose spent the first 20 years of his reign ruling alongside her – you'd think he might be a bit miffed about this, and maybe he was, because much later he tried to erase Hatshepsut's name from history.

VICTORY IN MEGIDDO

There had been no wars while Hatshepsut was in charge. But that changed when she died and Thutmose finally got to rule on his own. The princes of Kadesh and Megiddo, maybe trying their luck now that Hatshepsut was dead, got together and formed an uprising against him. They had made a big mistake. Thutmose marched his army across the Sinai desert to Gaza, then headed for Megiddo (in modern-day Israel). Instead of attacking by one of two more obvious routes, Thutmose chose to risk it and followed a winding, dangerous ravine. He took the enemy army by surprise and sent it running to the town of Megiddo, which

HARDOMETER

CUNNING: 9
COURAGE: 9
SURVIVAL SKILLS: 9
RUTHLESSNESS: 9

he besieged for seven months until it finally surrendered. Thutmose's glorious victory is recorded in the temple of Amun-Re at Karnak.

MORE GLORIOUS VICTORIES

For the next 18 years, Thutmose marched his army to Syria to make sure everyone got the message that he was very much in charge. He conquered new lands, including Nubia, and the kingdom of Mitanni – he was so pleased with conquering Mitanni that he held a huge celebration in Thebes. Modern historians have given Thutmose III the nickname 'the Napoleon of ancient Egypt' because of his constant military campaigns.

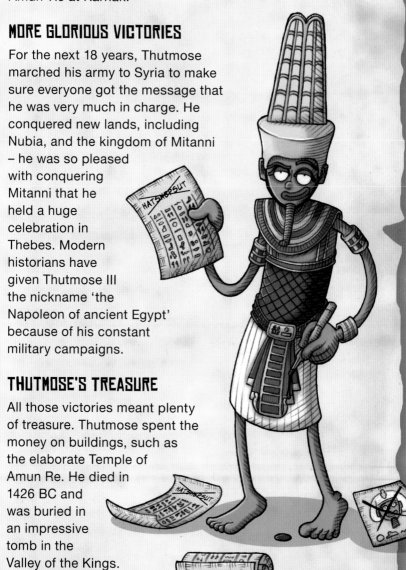

THUTMOSE'S TREASURE

All those victories meant plenty of treasure. Thutmose spent the money on buildings, such as the elaborate Temple of Amun Re. He died in 1426 BC and was buried in an impressive tomb in the Valley of the Kings.

THE AFTERLIFE GAME

For two to six players. You'll need a counter each and a dice to play this game.

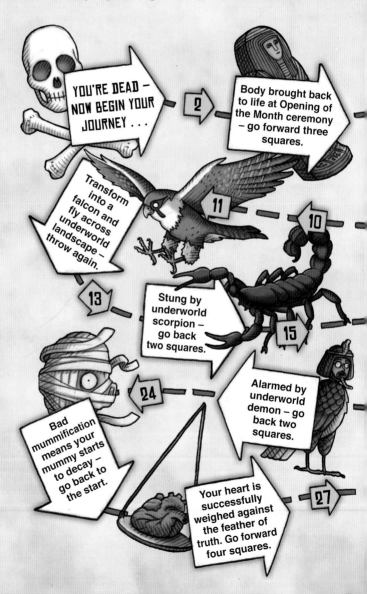

YOU'RE DEAD – NOW BEGIN YOUR JOURNEY . . .

2

Body brought back to life at Opening of the Month ceremony – go forward three squares.

Transform into a falcon and fly across underworld landscape – throw again.

11

10

13

Stung by underworld scorpion – go back two squares.

15

24

Alarmed by underworld demon – go back two squares.

Bad mummification means your mummy starts to decay – go back to the start.

Your heart is successfully weighed against the feather of truth. Go forward four squares.

27

Your mission is simple: everlasting life. First, you have to die, then your body has to be mummified and your funeral properly conducted. Then you have to find your way through the underworld using the spells in the Book of the Dead to help you. Good luck!

4

Attacked by a deadly snake in the underworld. Go back three squares.

6

Use a spell to turn into a crocodile – go forward five squares.

Fail to pacify underworld gateway god – miss a go.

8

17

18

Miss a go while you find the right spell to continue your journey.

Spell protects you against underworld demon – go forward two squares.

Fall down underworld cavern – go back five squares.

22

21

Your heart outweighs the feather and is eaten by the Devourer. You cease to exist.

29

Congratulations! You might join the gods, or you might go to a lovely land full of fields and rivers. Either way, everlasting life is yours!

SNEFRU

Snefru ruled at the end of the Old Kingdom, around four and a half thousand years ago. He built the first true pyramid, and it's still there today.

HARD NUT RATING: 7.5

SNEFRU'S NEW DYNASTY

Snefru began the fourth dynasty of Egyptian kings after he married the pharaoh's daughter and became pharaoh himself. He ruled such a long time ago that we don't know much about his reign, but ancient records show that Snefru led his warriors into Nubia, to the south of Egypt, where he captured treasure, and also raided the Libyans, to the west of Egypt. He might have used some of the prisoners of war he captured to fund and build his most famous legacy . . .

PYRAMID BUILDING

Snefru left something behind that has survived all the thousands of years since he lived: absolutely massive pyramids. Pyramids had been built before, built as tombs for the pharaohs of the third dynasty, but Snefru's were different. His first pyramid was originally built as a step pyramid, with its sides going upwards in steps, like the previous Egyptian pyramids. But Snefru changed his plans, making it a true pyramid with smooth sides. At some point, the pyramid collapsed, so we can see how it was built. The Bent Pyramid was Snefru's next attempt: it was designed as a true pyramid, but went a bit wrong, and when

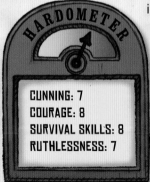

HARDOMETER

CUNNING: 7
COURAGE: 8
SURVIVAL SKILLS: 8
RUTHLESSNESS: 7

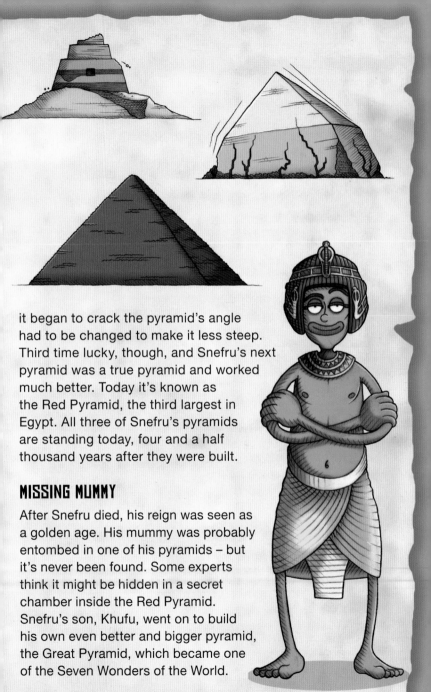

it began to crack the pyramid's angle had to be changed to make it less steep. Third time lucky, though, and Snefru's next pyramid was a true pyramid and worked much better. Today it's known as the Red Pyramid, the third largest in Egypt. All three of Snefru's pyramids are standing today, four and a half thousand years after they were built.

MISSING MUMMY

After Snefru died, his reign was seen as a golden age. His mummy was probably entombed in one of his pyramids – but it's never been found. Some experts think it might be hidden in a secret chamber inside the Red Pyramid. Snefru's son, Khufu, went on to build his own even better and bigger pyramid, the Great Pyramid, which became one of the Seven Wonders of the World.

INCREDIBLE EGYPTIAN PYRAMIDS

Pyramids were tombs for dead pharaohs, where the mummified king would find eternal life. Someone didn't just have the idea of building a gigantic four-sided triangular tomb one day – pyramids evolved over time . . .

EARLY GRAVES

In King Narmer's time (see page 10), the dead were buried in graves in the desert. Later the rich began to use coffins and sarcophagi (outer coffins).

GRANDER GRAVES

Gradually, tombs were given roofs and a structure above ground. They became more elaborate, and were filled with things that the dead person might need in the afterlife, so they needed a bit of underground storage. On top was a big block made out of rubble.

ZOSER'S PYRAMID

The pharaoh Zoser went a step further than having a big block of rubble on top of his tomb – in fact quite a few steps further. He built a stepped pyramid. Perhaps the idea was that the steps rising up to a pinnacle formed a stairway to heaven. Inside the pyramid a warren of tunnels and rooms surrounded Zoser's burial chamber.

PROPER PYRAMID

Snefru (see page 38) built the first pyramid with smooth sides instead of steps. It was 95 metres high, but the heavy outer layers slipped over time so it doesn't look much like a pyramid now. We can see from the pyramid that it started off as a stepped pyramid, but then the builders changed their minds. After that first attempt, Snefru managed to build a pyramid with flat sides that didn't collapse.

GREAT PYRAMID

The pharaoh Khufu built an absolutely enormous pyramid, known today as the Great Pyramid. It's 146.6 metres high, and you could fit St Paul's cathedral *and* the Houses of Parliament inside it and still have room to swing a cat. The Great Pyramid became one of the Seven Wonders of the World. It was already ancient by the time of the ancient Romans. The Great Sphinx – with a king's head and a lion's body 72 metres long – was built nearby, by Khufu's son Khaefre.

END OF THE PYRAMIDS

In the New Kingdom, pharaohs stopped building pyramids and instead built tombs in the Valley of the Kings (see page 26). But pyramids did continue to be built, and made a comeback with King Piye (see page 22) and his descendants.

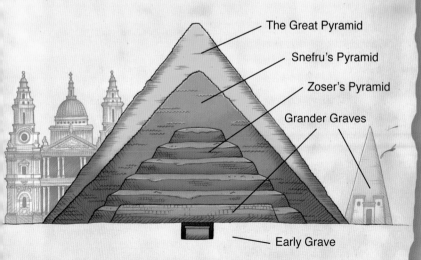

The Great Pyramid

Snefru's Pyramid

Zoser's Pyramid

Grander Graves

Early Grave

ESARHADDON

Esarhaddon was an invader: he was King of the Middle Eastern kingdom of Assyria, who conquered Egypt in the seventh century BC.

HARD NUT RATING: 8.5

MURDER AND MAYHEM

Although he wasn't the eldest son, Esarhaddon had been made the heir to the throne of Assyria by his father, the Assyrian King Sennacherib. Understandably, Esarhaddon's two older brothers weren't pleased that they'd been passed over in favour of their little brother. In fact, they were so angry that they murdered King Sennacherib and started a rebellion. Esarhaddon, who was just as cross as they were by this time, marched to meet them. He defeated his rebellious brothers and became King of Assyria in 680 BC.

REVOLTING NEIGHBOURS

Esarhaddon soon had new problems to deal with in the form of revolting leaders of neighbouring lands. He managed to sort them out with the help of a friendly neighbour who executed one of them – but he lost some of his northwestern lands to invaders.

HARDOMETER

CUNNING: 8
COURAGE: 9
SURVIVAL SKILLS: 8
RUTHLESSNESS: 9

INVADING EGYPT

Esarhaddon didn't have a minute's peace. The Egyptians started causing trouble in the city of Tyre, so Esarhaddon decided to do something drastic about it – he invaded Egypt in

675 BC. Four years later, he captured Memphis, and defeated the Egyptian king, Taharqa, a descendant of the Kushite King Piye (see page 22). Taharqa ran away, leaving the country to Esarhaddon.

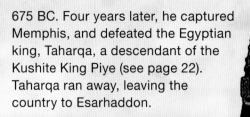

TAHARQA CAUSES TROUBLE

Esarhaddon celebrated becoming the first Middle Eastern king of Egypt, but he didn't stay there – instead he installed an Assyrian government, left it in the hands of Egyptian chiefs, and went back to Assyria. But once Esarhaddon had withdrawn his troops from Egypt, Taharqa popped up again, with quite a lot of support, and massacred the Assyrian troops who'd been left to stand guard.

ESARHADDON'S END

Esarhaddon was on his way to deal with Taharqa when he died, probably exhausted from all that invading and rebellion-crushing. Taharqa took control of Egypt for a while, but was finally defeated by Esarhaddon's son, and Taharqua ran away to Nubia. The Assyrians carried on ruling Egypt until it became part of the Persian Empire in 525 BC.

HATSHEPSUT

Hatshepsut was one of just a few female pharaohs. She grabbed power for herself, and hung on to it.

CHIEF WIFE

Hatshepsut was the chief wife of Thutmose II. Following the ancient Egyptian tradition for pharaohs, her husband was also her half-brother: their father was the pharaoh Thutmose I. Hatshepsut had a daughter but no sons, so Thutmose's heir was his son by a different wife. To make things simple (or possibly very confusing), he was also called Thutmose.

REIGNING AS REGENT

Thutmose II died in about 1479 BC when his son was still a child, so Hatshepsut ruled Egypt as Thutmose III's regent. But Hatshepsut was ambitious and after about seven years, she decided that being the most important woman in the whole of Egypt wasn't enough and had herself crowned pharaoh. Even when Thutmose was old enough to rule alone, she still continued to be joint pharaoh alongside him. Although she shouldn't really have been able to get away with it, somehow she did. She was given all the special titles and ceremonial dress that were due to a pharaoh, including the ceremonial false beard, which actually quite suited her!

TAKING A PUNT

Hatshepsut didn't wage any wars, although a temple painting suggests that she took part in a successful battle in Nubia. Instead of having lots of battles, Hatshepsut sailed to the land of Punt (which was probably in the area of modern day Ethiopia and Eritria, though no one's quite sure). Punt was famous for producing exciting things such as gold, ebony, exotic plants and aromatic spices and resins, all of which it traded with Egypt. Hatshepsut's expedition and Nubian campaign are recorded in the temple she built at Deir el-Bahri.

RUBBING OUT THE PAST

When Hatshepsut died in 1458 BC, her stepson was finally able to rule on his own. Much later, near the end of his reign, Thutmose III tried to remove Hatshepsut's name from the records. Maybe it was Thutmose's revenge after all those years of ruling with her, or maybe he wanted things to look nice and neat, with three Thutmoses in a row. He didn't succeed, though, and Hatshepsut is still well-known 3,500 years after her death.

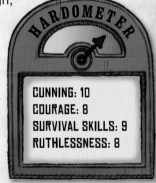

HARDOMETER

CUNNING: 10
COURAGE: 8
SURVIVAL SKILLS: 9
RUTHLESSNESS: 8

THE RIVER NILE

The River Nile is one of the two longest rivers in the world, flowing from its source in Central Africa to the Mediterranean Sea. Without it, Egypt would be a desert, and the ancient Egyptian civilisation would never have existed.

• The River Nile flows from south to north, which is unusual. That's why the north of the country was known as Lower Egypt and the south as Upper Egypt.

• Every year, the River Nile flooded, leaving behind lovely thick mud that made the land especially fertile making it easy for the Egyptians to grow plenty of food.

• In modern times, dams have been built so the Nile doesn't flood any more.

• The Nile is around 6,650 kilometres long. It's in competition with the Amazon in South America for the longest river in the world.

• The River Nile's mud made Egypt rich – plenty of food led to trade, and the building of towns, which eventually grew into a complex, wealthy civilisation.

• Most of the River Nile isn't in Egypt at all. It flows through ten different African countries, including Egypt. Only about a fifth of the Nile is actually in Egypt.

• The River Nile drains into the Mediterranean Sea at the Nile Delta in Lower Egypt – it spreads out over 240 kilometres of the coast. The land there is very fertile. In modern-day Sudan, the Nile splits in two: the White Nile and the Blue Nile. The White Nile is longer, and its source is still being debated – it's either in Rwanda or Burundi.

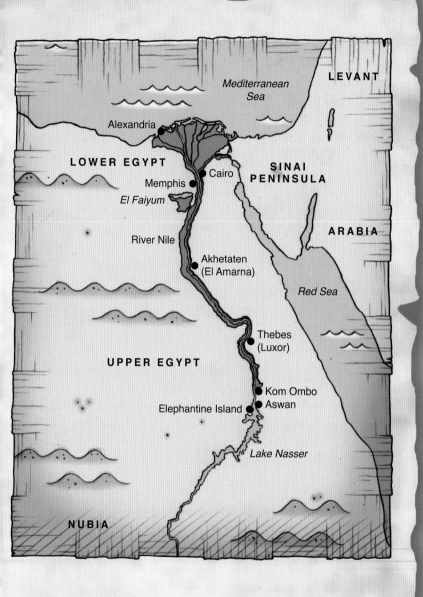

LEVANT

Mediterranean
Sea

Alexandria

LOWER EGYPT

Memphis ● Cairo

El Faiyum

SINAI
PENINSULA

River Nile

ARABIA

Akhetaten
(El Amarna)

Red Sea

Thebes
(Luxor)

UPPER EGYPT

Kom Ombo
Aswan

Elephantine Island

Lake Nasser

NUBIA

MENTUHOTEP II

Mentuhotep II defeated his enemies in the northern part of Egypt, reunited the country, and began the period of Egyptian history known as the Middle Kingdom.

HARD NUT RATING: 8.5

DIVIDED EGYPT

Mentuhotep was ruler of Upper Egypt around 4,000 years ago, with his capital at Thebes. Egypt was divided into two kingdoms at that stage, and for the previous 60 or so years, Mentuhotep's kingdom had been at war with the Heracleopolitan kingdom, to the north in Middle and Lower Egypt, with its capital at Heracleopolis. Each side struggled to conquer the other side and establish rule over the whole country.

SMITING ENEMIES

Mentuhotep made a determined attack on Heracleopolis when he'd been king for 14 years. Because the war was such a long time ago, we don't know much about it, but Mentuhotep might have been helped out a bit by a change of Heracleopolitan ruler that left his enemies vulnerable. Mentuhotep captured the city of Heracleopolis, no doubt involving an awful lot of smiting and bloodshed, and reunited Egypt. Nearly 4,000 years later, in the 1920s, archaeologists discovered a tomb near Mentuhotep's capital at Thebes. In it were 60 bodies of dead warriors, all of whom had been fatally wounded in battle,

HARDOMETER

CUNNING: 8
COURAGE: 9
SURVIVAL SKILLS: 8
RUTHLESSNESS: 9

and who are believed to be heroes who died fighting the Heracleopolitans.

CARRY ON FIGHTING

Thebes became the capital of the new, reunited Egypt. But Mentuhotep couldn't relax. He carried on fighting his old enemies in the north, and he also had to deal with raiders on the Nile delta. Still, he managed to find time to conquer the north of Nubia (to the south of Egypt), and to make a few other conquests elsewhere too.

WEALTHY EGYPT

Things were looking good for Mentuhotep and for Egypt – there was an increase in trade, things were better organised, and Egypt became richer as a united country. Mentuhotep used some of the cash to build new temples, and elaborate tombs for himself and his government officials. When he died around the middle of the 1900s BC, Mentuhotep left a united and wealthy country to his successor.

FIGHTING TO DO

CAMBYSES II

Cambyses II was a rampaging Persian conqueror who added Egypt to his vast empire in 525 BC.

HARD NUT RATING: 8

INHERITING AN EMPIRE

Cambyses' father, King Cyrus the Great, had conquered a mighty Persian Empire, which Cambyses inherited in 529 BC. While his father was still alive, Cambyses was governor of Babylonia (in modern-day Iraq). When his father was killed in battle with the Massagetae tribe, Cambyses took the opportunity to carry on his father's conquering policy.

INVASION PLANS

Cyrus had been planning to invade Egypt (he had plans for invading just about everywhere), and Cambyses decided he'd make Egypt part of the Persian Empire himself. He made alliances with the Arabs so that his army had enough supplies and water to cross the Sinai desert.

I SWEAR THIS IS THE LAST PLACE I HAD THEM...

PHARAOH CAMBYSES

Psamtik III, the Egyptian king, had only been on the throne for six months when Cambyses confronted his army at Pelusium, a city on the eastern Egyptian border in the Nile delta. Cambyses' Persian army defeated Psamtik easily, and Psamtik ran away to Memphis. But there was no escape. Cambyses besieged Memphis, captured the city, and took Psamtik prisoner. Psamtik was well treated at first, but later executed for conspiring against the Persians. The Persians now added Egypt to their already enormous empire. Cambyses became pharaoh, and took on the traditional dress and customs of Egyptian kings.

CAMBYSES' LOST ARMY

Cambyses had further plans for conquest and invaded the kingdom of Kush (modern-day Sudan), but had to return to Egypt when he ran out of supplies. He also sent an army from Thebes to conquer the Oasis of Amon, but having captured the Kharga Oasis, the whole army of 50,000 soldiers perished in a sandstorm in the Sahara Desert. People have been searching for Cambyses' lost army ever since.

MORE CONQUERING PLANS

Cambyses also had plans to attack Carthage, further west of Egypt, but a man claiming to be Cambyses' brother seized the Persian throne, and Cambyses was forced to return to Persia to sort things out. He didn't manage it, though – he died on the way, in 522 BC. No one is quite sure how he died – he might have had an accident, been murdered, or even killed himself. Darius the Great, a distant cousin, succeeded him.

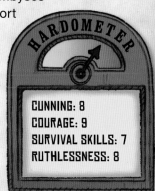

HARDOMETER

CUNNING: 8
COURAGE: 9
SURVIVAL SKILLS: 7
RUTHLESSNESS: 8

AHMOSE I

Ahmose I was an Egyptian warrior king who got rid of the foreign invaders, the Hyksos, for good.

HARD NUT RATING: 8.8

HYKSOS RULERS

Ahmose became king around 1550 BC, at the age of ten, when his father Seqenenre died (see page 18). The Hyksos, originally from Asia, had been ruling Egypt for about a hundred years, and Seqenenre had probably died trying to kick them out. Ahmose's task was to finish the war – hopefully by winning it.

YOUNG AHMOSE

In the early ears of Ahmose's reign, the Hyksos still had the upper hand, and might even have gained more land. But Ahmose was only ten, so expelling Asiatic overlords was probably a bit beyond him. His mother, Queen Ahhotep, ruled as regent while he was still young.

BASHING THE HYKSOS

Once Ahmose had grown up, things changed. He defeated the Hyksos allies in Middle Egypt and captured Memphis, the old capital of Egypt (near modern Cairo). Queen Ahhotep stayed in Thebes to defend it against the Hyksos. Meanwhile, Ahmose laid siege to the city of Avaris, the Hyksos capital in the eastern Nile delta. He had to make a quick trip to Upper Egypt to crush a rebellion, with the help of Ahhotep, but then he was back to finish the job

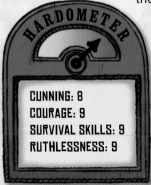

HARDOMETER

CUNNING: 8
COURAGE: 9
SURVIVAL SKILLS: 9
RUTHLESSNESS: 9

– he captured Avaris and chased the Hyksos north to the fortress of Sharuhen, near Gaza. After a three-year siege, he captured that too.

A BIT OF CONQUERING

Ahmose had finished what his father had started and kicked the Hyksos out of Egypt. So he decided to do a bit of conquering. The Nubian leader had been a friend of the Hyksos, so he marched his army into Nubia to teach the Nubians a lesson, but also to get his hands on the Nubian gold mines. He conquered Nubia, and went on the rampage in a different direction, conquering land in Syria too.

GONE FOR GOOD

Ahmose made sure all the people in power were loyal to him, and that trade was flourishing and industry booming. When he died, Egypt was reunited, free from invaders, and very prosperous. The Hyksos never returned to rule Egypt.

ANCIENT EGYPTIAN QUIZ

How much have you learned about the hard-nut ancient Egyptians, their customs, gods and enemies? Take this quiz and find out.

1. King Tutankhamun's mummy was unusual because it didn't contain his . . .

a) Brain

b) Heart

c) Tonsils

2. The god Anubis, god of embalmers, had the head of which animal?

a) A jackal

b) A hyena

c) A cheetah

3. What were canopic jars used for?

a) Storing spices

b) Storing mummies' insides

c) Storing the pharaoh's make-up

4. Which invader conquered Egypt in 525 BC?

a) King Cambyses II of Persia

b) King Piye of Kush

c) Alexander the Great

5. Hatshepsut was a female pharaoh. What did she wear to show she was an Egyptian king?

a) Horns, like the cow goddess Hathor

b) A pair of trousers

c) A false beard

6. Which Egyptian ruler had two powerful Roman boyfriends?

a) Nefertiti

b) Hatshepsut

c) Cleopatra

7. Which god had the head of an ibis?

a) Thoth

b) Bastet

c) Horus

8. Where was Tutankhamun buried?

a) In the Great Pyramid

b) In the Valley of the Kings

c) Underneath the Great Sphinx

9. Which foreign hard nuts did Ramesses the Great fight at the Battle of Kadesh?

a) The Assyrians

b) The Hyksos

c) The Hittites

10. To which goddess might you offer a mummified cat?

a) Nut

b) Bastet

c) Isis

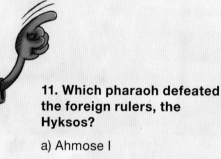

11. Which pharaoh defeated the foreign rulers, the Hyksos?

a) Ahmose I

b) Ptolemy I

c) Cleopatra

12. Which pharaoh built four gigantic statues of himself?

a) Thutmose III

b) Tutankhamun

c) Ramesses the Great

13. The Great Sphinx has the head of a pharaoh and the body of which animal?

a) A lion

b) A scorpion

c) A crocodile

14. Where might you find the Book of the Dead?

a) In a temple

b) Under the pharaoh's crown

c) In a coffin

15. Which king of Assyria conquered Egypt?

a) Apopis

b) Esarhaddon

c) Senachrib

HARD NUTS OF ANCIENT EGYPT TIMELINE

3200 BC

King Narmer lived around this time (this date and some of the others are a bit vague – but it all happened a very long time ago!).

2686 BC

The Old Kingdom began.

2670 BC

Zoser, who built the first stepped pyramids, ruled Egypt around this time.

2613 BC

Snefru, who built the first true pyramid, became pharaoh around this time.

2540 BC

The Great Pyramid was built by Khufu.

2181 BC

The Old Kingdom ended, and the Intermediate Period began, when minor kings were in power in Egypt.

2046 BC

Mentuhotep II reigned from around this date. He reunited Egypt and began the Middle Kingdom.

1900S BC

The Egyptians conquered Nubia.

1786 BC

The Middle Kingdom ended and the Second Intermediate Period began.

1663 BC

The Hyksos conquered Egypt and ruled for about a hundred years.

1560 BC

Reign of Seqenenre began around this date. He began rebelling against the Hyksos.

1550 BC

Ahmose I ruled from around this date. He defeated the Hyksos, and the New Kingdom began.

1479 BC

Thutmose III became pharaoh. A few years later, his stepmother and regent, Hatshepsut, became joint pharaoh.

1370 BC

Queen Nefertiti, wife of the pharaoh Akhenaten, was born around this date.

1336 BC

Tutankhamun began his short reign as king of Egypt.

1279 BC

Beginning of Ramesses the Great's reign as pharaoh.

1274 BC

The Battle of Kadesh, between the Egyptians and the Hittites took place.

MID-700S BC

Kushite King Piye invaded Egypt.

671 BC

Esarhaddon, King of Assyria, conquered Egypt.

525 BC

King Cambyses II conquered Egypt and made it part of the Persian Empire.

305 BC

Ptolemy I, Alexander the Great's general, became pharaoh and began a dynasty of Ptolemies.

51 BC

Cleopatra became pharaoh and ruled Egypt (with a brief interruption) until the Romans conquered Egypt.

30 BC

Egypt was conquered by the Romans, and became part of the Roman Empire.

GLOSSARY

ALLIANCE An agreement between different countries or nations to work together in order to achieve something

ANKH An ancient Egyptian symbol meaning 'life'

ASSASSIN Someone who kills people for political reasons

CANOPIC An ancient Egyptian jar used to hold the organs of embalmed bodies

CAVALRY Soldiers on horseback

DELTA Sand at the mouth of a river

DYNASTY A series of rulers from the same family

EMBALMED When a dead body is treated with chemicals in order to preserve it

EMPIRE A group of states or countries ruled by one leader or state

INFANTRY Foot soldiers

LEGACY Something handed down to future generations

OVERLORDS Particularly powerful lords

PALETTE A board or tray used to mix colours

PEACE TREATY An agreement between two parties to end war

PERILOUS Very dangerous

PLUNDERED Robbed of valuable goods

PROVINCES Regions of land that belong to a country or empire

REBEL Break away from (or resistance to) authority

RAVINE A small, steep valley

REGENT Someone who rules temporarily on behalf of the official ruler, when they can't rule themselves because they are too young or ill

REVOLTING Rebelling

SIEGE Surround a city or town with the aim of capturing it

SMITING Striking or hitting hard

STRONGHOLD A place that is well protected

VENOMOUS Poisonous

VULNERABLE Weak, and open to attack

WAGED Started

INDEX